MYTH OR MUST DO?

MYTH OR MUST DO?

Do you want to live a longer, healthier, and wealthier life?

Samuel Britton

iUniverse, Inc.
Bloomington

MYTH OR MUST DO?
DO YOU WANT TO LIVE A LONGER, HEALTHIER, AND WEALTHIER LIFE?

iUniverse books may be ordered through booksellers or by contacting:

iUniverse
1663 Liberty Drive
Bloomington, IN 47403
www.iuniverse.com
1-800-Authors (1-800-288-4677)

Because of the dynamic nature of the Internet, any web addresses or links contained in this book may have changed since publication and may no longer be valid. The views expressed in this work are solely those of the author and do not necessarily reflect the views of the publisher, and the publisher hereby disclaims any responsibility for them.

Any people depicted in stock imagery provided by Thinkstock are models, and such images are being used for illustrative purposes only.
Certain stock imagery © Thinkstock.

ISBN: 978-1-4620-4632-4 (sc)
ISBN: 978-1-4620-4631-7 (ebk)

Library of Congress Control Number: 2011914377

Printed in the United States of America

iUniverse rev. date: 08/27/2011

Do you want to live a longer, healthier AND wealthier life?

Here are some of the biggest financial, fitness and nutritional myths and the key building blocks to your success!

What is a myth? Webster's defines a myth as a person or thing's existence only in imagination, or whose actual existence is not verifiable.

I have been a financial advisor for over 15 years and a fitness and nutritional advisor in one form or another for much longer. The one astonishingly consistent thing that I have seen in both industries is that of people's preconceived notions of non truths based on no real evidence. Or simply put their belief in myths.

If I had a dollar for every debate I've had over these self-defeating fallacies, well, I could hire myself as a financial advisor. Ok, not so funny, but you get my point. Not only are these myths common to a very large majority of the people I meet with, but even more amazing is the conviction with which they hold onto them, regardless of facts to the contrary.

These myths have an immense influence on people's frame of reference, often to the point of sabotaging their desired outcomes. If it's investing, they're convinced they can effectively time the market or follow performance. When it comes to nutrition starving one's self or the latest and greatest fad diet is the way to go. My favorite, lifting weights causes women to get big and bulky, always causes me to laugh. People religiously follow these myths, much to the detriment of their financial and physical well being.

As Frank, a client and friend, recently said to me; "Sam you're a cockeyed optimist".

True to my nature, then I believe that if old habits die hard the good news is that they do die.

So in the interest of dispelling these myths I have put together 29 of the most common financial, fitness, and nutritional myths I've heard along with the truth behind the myth.

It is my sincere belief that if you change your thinking on even just a handful of these myths, you'll realize tremendous progress towards your goals in these areas.

This book is short, simple and combines health and wealth, two of the most important areas in a person's life. It is my hope that you will find this helpful to you.

FITNESS MYTHS

MYTH: Calories eaten after 8pm turn to fat.

This is one of my favorite myths. It does not matter what time you eat. Calories do not tell time. Whether you consume them during Good Morning America or Letterman, the simple fact is if you consume more calories than your body burns in a day, then you will gain weight.

Did you know??????
One pound=3500 calories
One gram of protein=4 Calories
One gram of carbohydrates=4 calories
One gram of alcohol=7 calories
One gram of fat=9 calories

MYTH: You inherit being overweight.

The science community has worked hard to identify the genes that potentially make us fat. According to the American Medical Association, less than 2% of obesity can be attributed to a genetic link. The truth is the larger problem lies in the bad habits we inherit, such as poor diet and lack of exercise.

The number of overweight Americans continues to grow.
-In 2009, 62.2% of adults in the U.S. were either overweight or obese. In 2010 that amount grew to 63.1% with a breakdown of 36.6% overweight and 26.5% obese.
For those of you wondering if a certain age group suffers from obesity
-18.3% young Americans
-27.6% between the ages of 30-44
-30.6% between the ages of 45-64
(Gallup-Heathway's Well Being Index)

MYTH: *Your metabolism slows down once you turn 30.*

Wrong! Studies upon studies have shown that the slowdown in metabolism is due to a loss in muscle tissue. The loss of muscle tissue is directly related to a lack of physical activity.

MYTH: *Spot reduction-1000 crunches a day will result in a flat stomach*

Spot reduction is quite simply just a myth. Unfortunately, this myth is a very effective way to trick uninformed people into buying lots of useless junk, mostly geared around abdominal equipment.

If you were to do 1000 crunches a day you will have beautifully ripped abs, however, they'll still be covered with that layer of fat. To actually see definition in your abs, men need a body fat content of between eight to ten percent and women about twelve to fourteen percent.[i]

You can't pick a specific body part to lose weight. Fat is lost proportionately throughout your body based on your genetic pattern. You reduce fat by creating a caloric deficit; you must train all of your muscles.

MYTH: Women should only do cardio, and if weight training, only lift light weights.

To begin with, if you only do cardio, your body will burn both fat *and* muscle as fuel. Also, weight lifting helps you to lose fat. The benefits of weight lifting are enormous, which we'll touch on later in this book. As for lifting light weights, that's also nonsense because muscle responds to resistance (overload) and if the resistance is too light, your body will not change.

Research has shown that after 20 weeks of training on Universal machines, women improved their muscular strength and defined their bodies, yet did not increase bone mineral density.

(Key to fighting osteoporosis)

MYTH: To build big muscles, I have to eat lots of protein.

If you want to build bigger muscles, two things are needed: Use enough weights to challenge your muscles beyond their normal resistance level, and take in more calories than you burn. Muscles work on calories, so you need all three types of nutrients, protein, carbohydrates and fats. While high protein diets are much the rave, the American Heart Association and the American Diet Association both recommend against such diets. The fear is of possible blood glucose abnormalities and nutrient imbalances. Plus, excess protein may be stored as fat. Your best approach to adding muscle mass is to enjoy a healthy eating and workout plan.[ii]

MYTH: The Cellulite myth

There really is no such thing as cellulite. The term cellulite actually refers to the dimpled and lumpy appearance of the skin that occurs when fat deposits sit just below the skin's surface. This fat is no different than other excess fat on the body. The best remedy is to keep a steady and healthy weight, eat lots of fruits, vegetables and other fibers, and exercise.

A balanced diet is not a cookie in each hand!

MYTH: As long as it's low fat or fat free, you can eat more.

Bottom line, losing or gaining weight comes down to the amount of calories that you consume, not how much fat you consume. Usually, when the fat is taken out, it is replaced by sugar or carbohydrates. This way the product can keep its taste. However, most of the time the caloric amounts are similar or even more. The big problem usually comes from people thinking that they can consume extra helpings due to the fat free labels.

USDA (United States Department of Agriculture) dietary recommendations for daily fiber are 25 grams for women and 38 grams for men.

These numbers are meant for people with active lifestyles consuming over 2000 calories per day.

The British minimum fiber guidelines are 12 and 24 grams daily.[iii]

MYTH: All fats are bad.

Fats are an essential part of the diet. The USDA actually recommends that around 30% of total daily caloric intake comes from fat (Less than 10% should come from saturated fat).

However, not all fats are created equal. So, try to replace bad fats (Saturated fats and Trans fats) which cause heart disease and certain types of cancers, with good fats.

Some examples of good fats would be Olive Oil, Nuts, Seeds and Omega 3 (which is found in fish).

Some of their many benefits include helping with the absorption of nutrients, maintaining heart and cardiovascular health, maintaining cell membrane integrity, as well as containing anti-inflammatory properties. They may also act as an anti-depressant.

Be sure to remember that fats are higher in calories and when consumed in excess will contribute to weight gain.

MYTH: *Weight training turns fat into muscle, and if you stop working out the muscle turns back to fat.*

This is like saying that you can turn rocks into diamonds. If this was possible, think of the advantage that a heavier person would have over a thinner person.

Fat cannot turn into muscle and muscle cannot turn into fat. You gain muscle by weight training and you lose fat through aerobics and diet.

What can be confusing is when a person stops weight lifting they lose muscle (shrinks) due to inactivity. They usually couple that with poor diet. Combine poor eating habits and a slowed metabolism (less activity) and less muscle mass and what you have is the appearance of muscle turning to fat, but in reality, muscle is being lost and fat accumulated.

MYTH: *Women lose weight faster than men.*

Actually, the opposite is true. Unfair as it may be, men lose weight faster than women.

1   First off, men have more muscle which allows them to burn more calories.

2   Men respond quicker to exercise. A woman's body will go into starvation mode, slowing her metabolism in an effort to retain fat. This is because women have higher levels of estrogen. (A hormone responsible for retaining fat to help with pregnancy)

3   Women often feel as if they are working out harder than men, even if both are at the same level simply because a woman's lung capacity is smaller.[iv]

MYTH: Machines are just as good as free weights

The origination of exercise machines was to make exercising easier. That should be your first red flag. Exercise is not supposed to be easy. The truth is that free weights are better. Free weights use stabilizing muscles that machines do not, therefore, you engage more muscle fibers with more contractions. Weight training also increases bone mass which, in turn, decreases the potential for osteoporosis.

By the way, did you know that the primary reason seniors enter a nursing facility is due to a decline in muscle and bone mass.

People get old and die. Not true, most people get old and live

Myth: *Women's weight training will make me "bulk up"*

Whenever I put together a workout plan for women, the very first thing that I hear is "I prefer to avoid weight lifting because I don't want to bulk up". Sometimes I'll get the negotiator who's willing to give the pink dumbbells a try.

Ladies listen up!!! The fact is that women do not produce as much testosterone (one of the main hormones responsible for increasing muscle size) as men do. Therefore it is impossible for women to build large amounts of muscle naturally. Most women don't have the problem of building too much muscle; it's that they haven't got enough muscle.

Research has shown the benefits of strength training over and over.

1) You will be physically stronger: Even moderate strength training has shown to increase a woman's strength by 30-50%.

2) Lose body fat: The average woman who strength trains two times per week for two months will gain almost two pounds of muscle and lose three and a half pounds of fat.

3) You decrease the risk of Osteoporosis: Six months of strength training has shown to increase bone density by as much as thirteen percent. Add in dietary calcium and you have a strong defense against Osteoporosis.

4) Reduce the risk of Heart Disease and Diabetes: Weight training promotes cardiovascular well being which in turn helps fight off many diseases as well as lowering bad Cholesterol (LDL) and increasing good Cholesterol (HDL).

In the case of Diabetes, more muscle and less fat will improve the utilization of sugar from the bloodstreams.

5) Improved overall attitude: A Harvard study revealed that ten weeks of strength training greatly improved feelings of confidence and overall capability of people suffering from depression above that of standard counseling.

6) Benefits to seniors: Studies have also shown that women in their seventies and eighties have seen significant strength buildup after weight training.

Finally ladies, since muscles take up less room than fat, weight training will help you **lose inches** and **look better**.

MYTH: Exercising a certain way will give you toned muscles.

Muscles can do four things, they contract, they expand, they grow, and they shrink. That's it. You can't specifically do anything to "shape or tone" a muscle.

What most people believe to be toned is actually a combination of two things, training for muscle growth (increased resistance) and lowering body fat (aerobics and watching caloric intake).

MYTH: *The Kelly and Ann Marie myth: Negative calories.*

The negative calories phrase refers to foods (fruits and vegetables) that contain such a small amount of calories that the body uses more energy to digest and absorb them. This means that when eating these foods alone there is a potential for a net loss of calories from the body.

While this is not really a myth, it is in need of clarification. Recently after explaining to friends Kelly and Ann Marie, that by eating an apple for a snack they would consume 85 calories however, it would take 95 calories to digest that apple, they felt that if they ate enough apples they would build up extra credit to have a bigger piece of cake. HAHA!

Some excellent negative calorie foods are:

Asparagus, Broccoli, Carrots, Celery, Lettuce, Spinach, Clementines, Grapefruit, Cantaloupe, Peaches and Plums.

Skip at a price!
A University of Massachusetts study found that those who regularly skip breakfast are four and a half times more likely to be obese.[v]

MYTH: I sweat during my workout because I'm out of shape.

The first thing to know is that sweating is how your body cools off. As your metabolic heat begins to increase, there is a rise in your core temperature activating sweat glands. Next, fluid is transferred to the skin and evaporates, thus causing a cooling effect. Many things can cause either a fit person or an out of shape person to sweat, such as room temperature, body temperature, genetics, or maybe the clothes that you're wearing.

How much cholesterol per day can I have? Answer 300mg

How much sodium per day can I have? Answer 2400-3000mg[vi]

MYTH: If I starve myself I'll lose weight.

This one is at the top of the list when it comes to mistakes made for losing weight.

When you restrict your caloric intake you slow your metabolic rate. This is called **starvation mode**. It is real and well documented: The Minnesota study is one of the most famous studies in this area and they found when a person restricts their calories by up to 50% their metabolic rate slowed by 40%.

On top of this, the health risks can be enormous, such as reduced immune system, fatigue, and potential eating disorders.

Did you know the World Health Organization classifies any diet under 1800 calories for women and 2200 for men per day as a starvation diet?

The starvation diet is almost always a recipe for weight loss and health disasters

The answer is to eat five to six smaller well balanced meals per day. You will speed up your metabolism, burn more calories, its much healthier, and it's a proven weight loss strategy. Not to mention you won't be hungry all day.

If you eat 5 to 6 smaller meals a day and exercise you will reach your goals.
If you make this a way of life you'll keep your goals.[vii]

FAD DIETS

MYTH: *The latest fad diet works!*

Quick fix weight loss programs are everywhere. They claim to have all the answers on easy weight loss. There are time specific diets, and food specific diets. Low calorie diets, and high protein low carbohydrate diets. The list is long and the worst part is, most people know they really don't work. So why do so many people turn to these kind of diets if they know they don't work? Some are looking for the easy way and unwilling to commit to what it takes. Many are frustrated at having failed in previous attempts to lose weight.

How will I know a fad diet?

Usually, they restrict or advocate a certain food group. They make scientific claims that have no supporting truth whatsoever, like claims of rapid weight loss, maybe within 10 days or so. Or programs that boast of chemical reactions within the body boosting your metabolism and weight loss.

Dangers of Fad Diets

Most of these diets are just not nutritionally sound. They recommend eating only specific foods, therefore, depriving us of important vitamins and minerals that are essential to our overall health.

Combo Diets

These are based on protein, carbohydrate and fat intake, for example, using higher amounts of protein while restricting carbohydrates. Some of the more popular diets in this area are the Atkins Diet, Scarsdale Diet, South Beach Diet, and the Kimkins Diet Plan.

One particular food:

The focus of these diets is to eat one particular food for a set amount of days or meals. Familiar names are the Cabbage Soup Diet, Chicken Soup Diet, Chocolate Chip Cookie Diet, "Are you kidding me" and the Popcorn Diet.

Specific day and time diets:

These diets will direct you towards what to eat, at what time to eat, and on what day. You may have heard of the Moon Diet, and the 7 Day All You Can Eat Diet.

The fact is that 95% of all fad diets fail!!!! That is why setting weight loss as a goal is a poor idea.

FINANCIAL MYTHS

<u>MYTH:</u> *I need to know which stocks to buy and when to buy them to make money.*

This is not correct. Academic studies have demonstrated that asset allocation is responsible for 93% of investor returns. Only 2% is actually related to market timing and 5% to security selection.

What's so interesting is that Wall St. has long been advocating what stocks to buy and when. In reality it doesn't amount to much.

What does have a much greater chance of helping you reach your financial goals is a proper asset allocation.[viii]

Money is better than poverty if only for financial reasons.
Woody Allen

<u>MYTH:</u> Performance will show you where to invest.

It is amazing to me how many people base their investment decisions solely on performance. This is almost always a disaster. To begin with, the performance is usually attributable to which market sectors have been in favor. Market sectors are cyclical and what's up can quickly go down. With this type of investment strategy investors chasing performance typically buy at or near the peak, missing most of the upside and positioning themselves for the downturn. For the future, try viewing performance as a measurement towards your targeted goals

MYTH: My investments advisors job is to find me opportunities.

If your advisor is constantly coming to you with the latest great opportunity, you may have more of a commission oriented salesman than an actual advisor. The job of an investment advisor is to develop a financial model to meet the client's needs, to provide discipline and guidance throughout the process, and to be the separation between your money and your emotions.

The magic of compound interest.

Imagine a job offer of work lasting exactly 31 days. You are given the choice of a flat $474,836 or a daily wage starting with one penny on the first day and then doubling each day.

Which would you choose?

I hope you took the penny because at the end of 31 days the amount would be $21,474,836.

Day 1: $.01

Day 2: $.02

Day 3: $.04

Day 4: $.08

Day 5: $.16

Day 6: $.32

Day 7: $.64

Day 8: $1.28

Day 9: $2.56

Day 10: $5.12

Day 11: $10.24

Day 12: $20.48

Day 13: $40.96

Day 14: $81.92

Day 15: $163.84

Day 16: $327.68

Day 17: $655.36

Day 18: $1,310.72

Day 19: $2,621.44

Day 20: $5,242.88

Day 21: $10,485.76

Day 22: $20,971.52

Day 23: $41,943.04

Day 24: $83,886.08

Day 25: $167,772.16

Day 26: $335,544.32

Day 27: $671,088.64

Day 28: $1,342,177.28

Day 29: $2,684,354.56

Day 30: $5,368,709.12

Day 31: $10,737,418.24

Day 32: $21,474,836.48

*Example used for illustrative purposes only

MYTH: A portfolio invested 100% in bonds is the safest investment.

This is not necessarily true and needs qualifying. The bond market is subject to interest rate risk, meaning that bond prices will drop as interest rates rise. When purchasing a bond you will receive a fixed rate of return for a fixed time period. If interest rates rise from the date of purchase, the bond will have to trade at a discount in order to reflect the lower return received.

There's also a default risk in which the issuer is unable to meet their obligation. Call risk which allows the issuer to retire a bond at a higher interest rate and issue a new bond at a lower rate, and inflation risk, which simply means if your bond is yielding 3% but interest rates are at 4%, you'll be able to buy less with the proceeds.

One possible answer is to shorten the duration of the bonds. Bonds with short term maturities are less volatile than those of longer term maturities. Another, is to spread the risk with multiple holdings. Perhaps most importantly, particularly in unusual interest rate environments, a diversified portfolio may help to serve you best.

MYTH: *Social Security and Medicare running out of money.*

This one may not be all myth, but in the case of social security, trustees responsible for projecting the future size of the trust fund believe the system will not run out of money.

The latest projections by the chief actuary have 2037 as the year funds are exhausted, even if no changes are made to the current system. However, experts feel that the calculations are extremely conservative. A second projection using numbers closer to the average found the trust fund would have over 14 trillion dollars in 2037. Originally, when social security was started in the 1930's, life expectancy for a woman was 63 and for a man, 59. Today those numbers are 85 and 82. This explains part of the problem.

Unfortunately, the news on Medicare is less optimistic. Currently we are using principal and the program will exhaust all funds in 2017.[ix]

MYTH: Men are from Mars and Women are from Venus sure, but when it comes to investing, we think alike

Wrong again. You can add investing to the list of differences. When it comes to investing, women are more likely to seek professional advice while men are most likely to go it alone. Women will do their research and for men it's more of trial and error. Women like steady growth with less income and man's motto is "I'll take some risk with that portfolio". Men however, are more likely to rebalance their portfolio, which is vital when managing risk. Obviously these are generalizations, not all men and women fall into these categories. I'll leave it to you to decide.[x]

People on average spend more time planning their vacations than their finance

MYTH: *I use the media as my window to the investment world*

Well, try closing the shades more often. Many people believe that the best advice for investing comes from the media. The media, which is a highly competitive industry, like all business, is trying to make a profit. In order to accomplish this they need to attract an audience. A task made easier the more dramatic the material. The focus is put on an extreme, negative or positive. Create an over bleak picture of the economy or overly hype the slightest bit of good news. Just enlarge whatever economic swings are in place. This causes investors to react to short term circumstance based on distorted perceptions, the result of emotions like fear and greed.

In order to truly take control of your financial future you need a well built financial strategy and the commitment to see it through.

Samuel Britton

MYTH: Foreign creditors could wipe out the US Treasury overnight.

This is another popular one. I wish I had a dollar for every time I've heard someone say that Japanese, Chinese, and other foreign investors are buying up our country (US Treasury) and when they sell we'll be left in complete chaos.

Right now foreigners own 4.3 trillion of Treasury debt. The top three are China, Japan and The United Kingdom, in that order. Oil exporters and Caribbean Banking Centers are also in the top six. Of the 4.3 figure, 1.1 trillion is with private investors, mostly pension funds and institutional investors.

People seem to think that it's bad business for the rest of the world to lend money to the US. However, looking at the facts, this is an investment that is absolutely liquid, has never defaulted, and is backed by the full faith of the US government. On top of that with so many different investors, just who decides to make this grand scale liquidation?

Caribbean Banking Centers include Bahamas, Bermuda, Cayman Islands, Netherlands and the British Virgin Islands.

Oil exporters include Ecuador, Venezuela, Indonesia, Bahrain, Iran, Iraq, Kuwait, Saudi Arabia, The United Arab Emirates, Algeria, Gabon, Libya and Nigeria.[xi]

54% of American workers report having less than $25,000 in savings and investments, and 27% have less than $1,000 saved.[xii]

MYTH: Real Estate is the safest and best investment.

So far as the best investment, it's highly unlikely that real estate will generate high enough returns to substantially impact your wealth. As far as real estate being the safest investment, it's barely worth mentioning how false that myth is after this last recession.

Now please understand that I think buying a primary residence is possibly the best move for your financial future. Buying second homes, rental properties, commercial property, etc. is where you may need to take another look.

The stock market has outperformed real estate almost 2 to 1 historically, and that's before you begin backing out after tax interest expense from the mortgage, title costs, maintenance, insurance, furnishings, and well, you get the picture.

Try not to get confused by the developers who buy very cheaply and are highly leveraged or companies that are actually making money off of their business or possibly raising stock.

The average return on real estate from 1963 through 2010 was 5.49%. The average return for the S&P over the same time period was 12.28%.[xiii]

Leveling off? At the end of 2008, 8% of mortgages had at least 1-payment past due and another 3% of mortgages were in foreclosure. At the end of 2009, 10% of mortgages were late and another 5% were in foreclosure. As of March 31st 2010, 9% of mortgages were late and 5% were in foreclosure. (Mortgage Bankers Association 2010)

MYTH: Do not invest internationally because of the risk.

Most people believe that when they invest internationally they get a country with an unstable government and no real financial stability. They see these companies producing some obscure product for a small corner of the world.

While political, economic and currency fluctuations are a consideration, the efficient frontier (the science of risk efficient portfolios) shows us that by adding between 5% (conservative) and 25% (aggressive) internationally, depending on your goals and risk tolerance, actually decreases the amount of risk to a portfolio.

This type of thinking may have had a case back in 1970 when only 34% of the world's market capitalization was of non US companies. However, by 2003 the market capitalization of non US companies had grown to 56% surpassing the US. Furthermore, predictions are that by 2036 foreign markets will represent 70% of the value of all worldwide investments, yet most US investors have less then 15% exposure to non US companies.[xiv]

MISSED OPPORTUNITIES

Out of the worlds 10 largest

Companies, the following are **NON** US based

10 out of 10 **Construction & Housing Companies**

10 out of 10 **Misc. Materials & Commodity Companies**

10 out of 10 **Shipping Companies**

9 out of 10 **Steel**

8 out of 10 **Automobile Companies**

8 out of 10 **Building Materials & Components Companies**

8 out of 10 **Insurance Companies**

7 out of 10 **Appliance & Household Durables Companies**

7 out of 10 **Banking Companies**

7 out of 10 **Beverages & Tobacco Companies**

xv

MYTH: *Timing the market*

So many people believe that the key to successful investing is getting in and out of the market at the right time. They try to figure out where will stocks be in 3 months? How about oil? Real Estate?

The fact is that investors who try to concentrate on market timing are fooling themselves. Jumping in and out of the markets is not a reliable strategy for wealth creation or risk management.

For example, $10,000 invested into the S&P 500 on Jan 1st 1980 was worth $121,029 on June 30th of 2008. If you backed out the ten best performing days over that time frame (7,192 days) the value drops to $70,745. That's 42% less.

If you were to miss the 50 best performing days your average annual return would have been less than 1%.[xvi]

Missing the Market[*]

S&P 500 Index:

December 31,1994-December 31, 2004

Period of Investment	Average Annual Total Return	Growth of $10,000
Fully Invested	12.07%	$31,260
Missed the 10 best days	6.89%	$19,476
Missed the 20 best days	2.89%	$13,414
Missed the 30 best days	-0.39%	$9,621
Missed the 40 best days	-3.19%	$7,233
Missed the 60 best days	-7.90%	$4,390

[*]FactSet Research Systems, Inc.

Successfully timing the market would not only require predicting the future, but also require, making changes in a cost effective manner (fees/taxes).

Investors, especially new ones, tend to gauge investing on their most recent experience, with emotion being a decision maker.

A better answer would be to build an asset allocation strategy in line with your goals. Remember asset allocation is responsible for about 93% of the performance in your portfolio.

Rebalance to keep yourself on track!!
and
Have patience!!

There is a saying in my business which I believe is very true, "it's less important to do something brilliant and far more meaningful not to do something stupid".

PHILOSOPHY OF INVESTING

"Time in the market, not market timing."

"The conclusion is fairly clear . . . . unless a manager can predict whether the market will be good or bad each year with considerable accuracy (e.g. be right at least seven out of ten), he should probably avoid attempts to time the market altogether."

William F. Sharpe

Nobel Peace Prize Winner in Economic Sciences 1990

(Developed the Sharpe Ratio for Measuring Risk and author of

"Likely Gains from Market Timing")

"They know of no firm or individual investor who has been successful in predicting the market even as much as 50 percent of the time."

David L. Babson and Thomas E. Babson

"There is an even greater disservice to the investing public than the more obvious hocus-pocus put forth in price guessing. It leads uninformed investors into believing that the one prerequisite of investing success is anticipating market movements. It encourages them to try to do what experience shows cannot be done, rather than to follow sound basic principles that have proved to be extremely effective over the years."

David L. Babson and Thomas E. Babson

"Focus on consistency over the long-term"

"In investment management, the real opportunity to achieve superior results is not in scrambling to outperform the market, but in establishing and adhering to appropriate investment policies over the long term-policies that position the portfolio to benefit from riding with the main long-term forces in the market. Investment policy, wisely formulated by realistic and well informed clients with a long-term perspective and clearly defined objectives, is the foundation upon which portfolios should be constructed and managed over time and through market cycles. In reality, very few investors have developed such investment policies."

Charles D. Ellis, author "The Elements of Investing

"Serious investors should avoid timing markets"
David Swensen, Chief Investment Officer of the Yale University endowment

"The odds against market timing are huge!"
Larry E. Sedroe in his book, "What Wall Street Doesn't Want You to Know"

In closing, I'd like to share a story with you . . .

Harvard University

Class of 1979 study concludes

In this study, a poll was taken of the graduating class to see how many students actually had a plan in place for their future. Surprisingly, only 3% of the class had a plan.

Ten years later they revisited that class and found that the 3% with a plan in place were earning on average 10 times as much as the other 97% of the class put together that had no plan.[xvii]

Planning = SUCCESS

Only one retiree in six has a written plan

16% have a written plan

48% have an informal plan

36% have no plan at all [xviii]

If you want to live a long, healthy, and prosperous life then you should consider living according to these priorities.

i.   The American Council on Exercise 2010.

ii.   American Heart Association/American Diet Association 2010.

iii. Department of Exercise and Nutrition Sciences, University at Buffalo. UPP members, Buffalo Health and Science Chapter 2010.

iv.   Medical Science Sports and Exercise, April 2008
      Sex Differences in Pulmonary Function during Exercise.

v.   Yunsheng MA. PHD 1994-1998.
      University of Massechusetts Medical School 1994-1998

vi.   USDA recommendations 2010.

vii. Source: Wikipedia The Free Ecyclopedia
      Minnesota Starvation Experiment Nov. 19 1944-Dec. 20 1945

viii. 1999 Source: Ibbotson Associates. Authors- Roger Ibbotson, Chairman of Ibbotson Associates and Yale Financial Professor, & Paul Kaplan, VP and Chief Economist at Ibbotson Associates 1999.

      Study: Does Asset Allocation Policy Explain 40% 90% or 100% of performance? 1999.

      1986 Source: Gary Brinson, L Randolph Hood and Gilbert Beebower Academic Study 1986.

ix.   Source: Treasury Department/Health and Human Services Department.

x.   Source: Journal of Financial Planning March 2, 2000 issue. A Study of Financial Beliefs and Behaviors February 2000.

xi. Source: Department of Treasury/Federal Reserve Board. November 16, 2010

xii. Employee Benefit Research Institute's 2010 Retirement Confidence Survey

xiii. Source: moneychimp.com

xiv. Source: bespokeinvest.typepad.com
www.straightstocks.com

xv. Source: Rimes Technologies Corp. (Constituents of MSCI All Country World Index)

xvi. Bloomberg

xvii. The book "What They Don't Teach You in the Harvard Business School" by Mark McCormick 1989. Harvard MBA Statistics page.

xviii. Source LIMRA. The Retirement Income Reference Book/Oct 23, 2009

The information contained herein is based on data from multiple sources and no representation is made as to the accuracy or completeness of data from outside sources. The information and data provided in this book is as of the date the book was written and is subject to change without notice.

This book has been prepared for informational purposes only. It does not provide individually tailored investment advice. It has been prepared without regard to the individual financial circumstances and objectives of persons who receive it. The appropriateness of a particular investment or strategy will depend on an investor's individual circumstances and objectives.

This book may not be construed as providing tax or legal advice. Individuals should consult their personal tax and legal advisors before making any related decisions.

This book has also been prepared without regard to the individual's health and fitness circumstances and objectives. Individuals should consult their doctor before making any related decisions.